Scarce

DWIGHT DRUMMOND

Ordering Information:

For orders and inquiries, please contact:
1-888-404-1388
www.goldtouchpress.com
book.orders@goldtouchpress.com

Printed in the United States of America

Contents

Scarce

Preface:
Scarce foretell the Literary discussions of Religion.

Description:
Scarce explores the Literary components of Religion.

ISOLATED
GENDER
DIFFERENCE
ETHNICITY
PREJUDICE
BLACK
WHITE
DISCRIMINATION
RACISM
APATHETIC
MINORITY
BIGOTRY INTOLERANCE

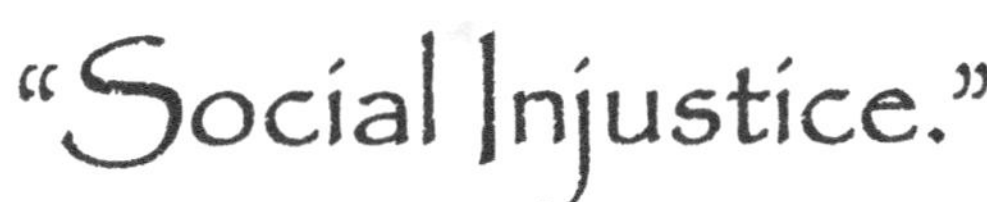

"Social Injustice."

Social demonstration of Mental withdraw helpful to none once the devastation that they have caused. Once knowledge now damage to everyone in sight. I have come to know that most Relatives are Guilty for exploitation with informative gestures when shouldn't be brought out to public light.

"I HAVE A DREAM"

"Civil Discrimination."

Civil Discrimination of verbal demonstration in Justice,
what are the facts that will push us forward to be unlike ourselves with
weakness and more protective to each choice we make as People.

“Relative Paparazzi.”

Relatives provoked by Jealously consumed from envy that snare traps
forced in trickery. They soon will come to Understand with all
Hatred pushes forth the need toward Change....."

"Relative Paparazzi."

"Scarce."

When necessity awaken, the inner most depth of solidarity see it necessary to ignore being safe toward People who are "Scarce."

Even without importance the reality of Life should be permissive to the wayward agenda for a Man in withstanding the reality in Life........."

"Blacative."

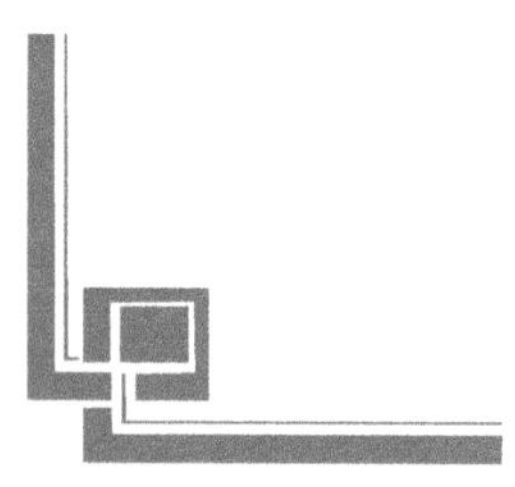

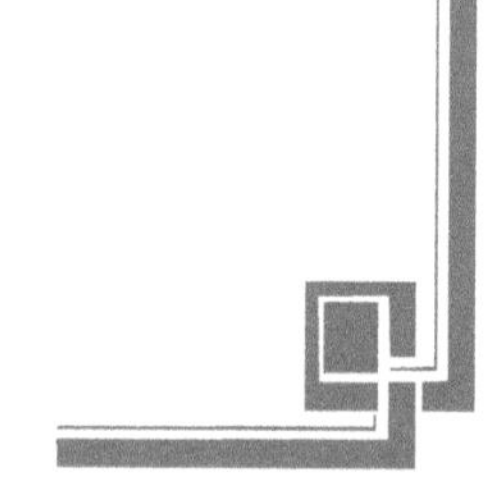

"Black Stars of David."

Those written within the Biblical perspective of those who would understand not to realize what wasn't explained in the artifacts of History.........."

"Black stars of David."

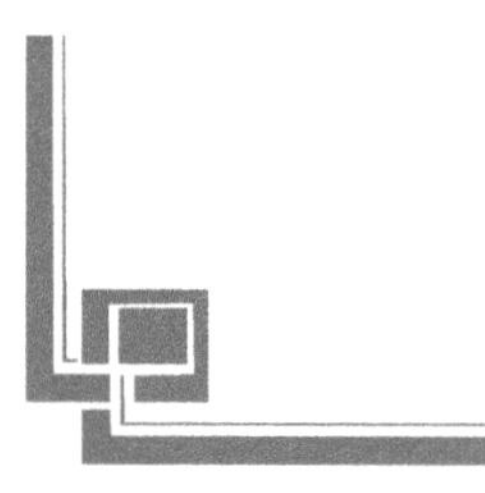

ZEPPELIN

"Elias."

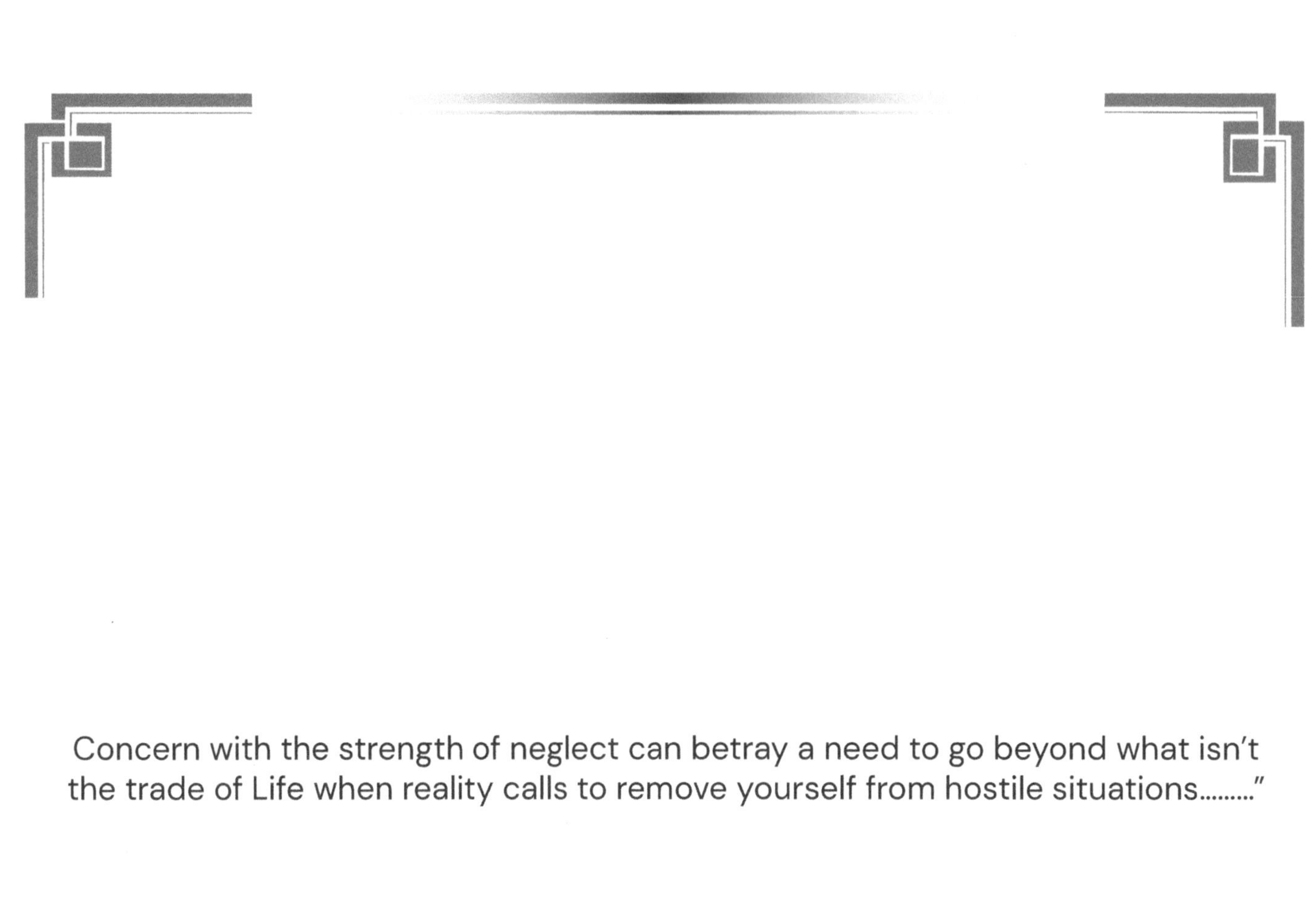

Concern with the strength of neglect can betray a need to go beyond what isn't the trade of Life when reality calls to remove yourself from hostile situations………"

"Aaron."

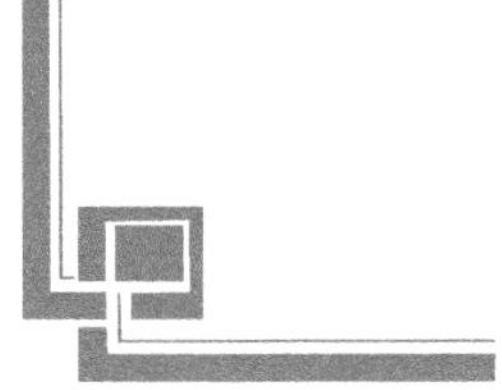

In outward situations what gives those the position to do without Prayer in times of need when every reality for Life pushes against the stone in strife........."

"Aaron."

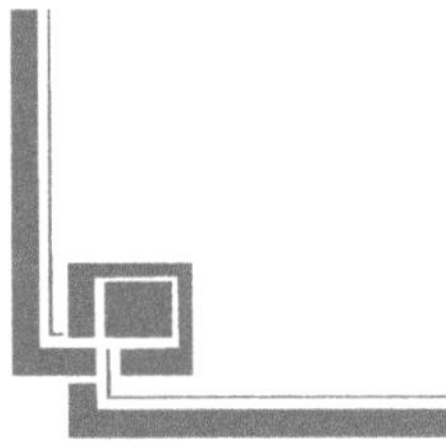

"Thumbprint."

Conspiracy reacts to the need in being without a answer when nothing else matters in proof of not believing reality but in need to produce any answer........."

"Thumbprint."

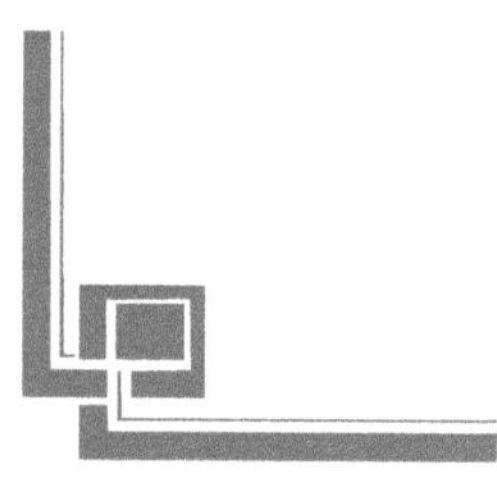

"Vive."

When importance causes those around you to remove what isn't necessary for those who don't know that things are reality toward the facts of not knowing that "Vive." Is supposed to be......."

"Salome."

From Peace her name reigns within objects of knowing that she is a woman.........."

"Salome."

"Sweet Liar."

As she strengthens the areas of importance many see it reason
for her not to tell the Truth......."

"Sweet Liar."

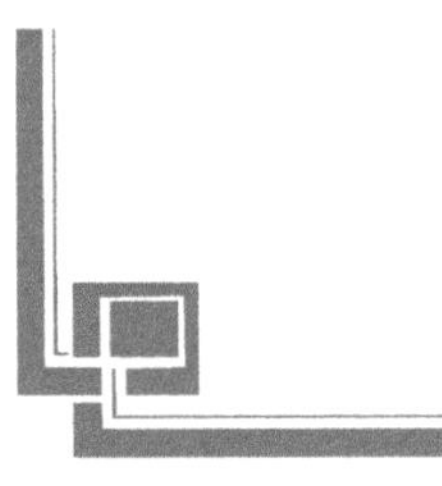

"Ghetto Tongues."

Jesus was born in the slums and folly of Galilee and taught Jerusalem principles who would never demeanor the activity toward humility.......''

ZEPPELIN

"Turquoise Diamond"

In the clarification of this Diamond I realized to never take advantage
of nothing that is Beautiful......."

"Turquoise Diamond."

WELL
DONE

"Dunaway."

Dunaway with undiscovered notions covered by the wayward
acts of civility which never changes........."

"Rabbi & Reason."

Every reason is given decision to be unkind to those who are given
Religious Position to be unlike us........."

"Rabbi & Reason."

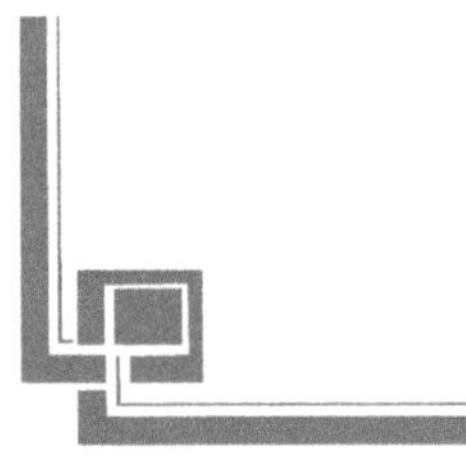

"Mistaken."

Mistaken is the belief that stress seems to be important which never matters toward every will of strength. When Life seems so weak never fall for folly, when the world is so defeated think again success………"

"Unto Jacob."

Unto Jacob the Blessing rely in Perseverance which allows
many to not take advantage of inheritance………"

"Life Reflections"

Sometimes in Life the cause of intervention allow others to think
beyond Life will of Privacy………"

"Life Reflections."

"Remember Esau."

Remember those who lay beyond the foundation from where Reality comes with at the cost of being railroaded by Truth wayward reaction………"

"Remember Esau."

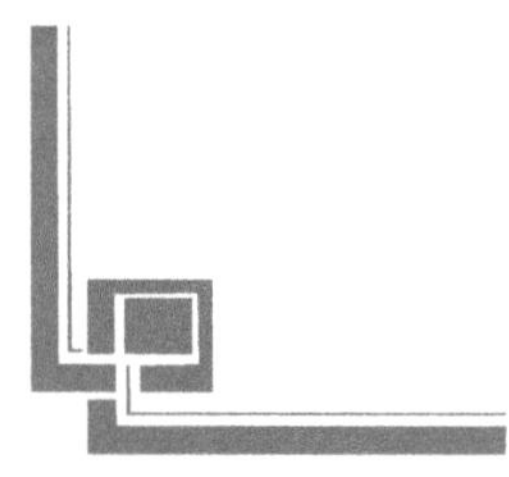

THY
PRAYERS &
THINE ALMS ARE
COME UP
BEFORE GOD

"Cornelius."

In Biblical perspective a cause distant from the original cause of what doesn't matters to those who doesn't care about Scripture………"

"Cornelius."

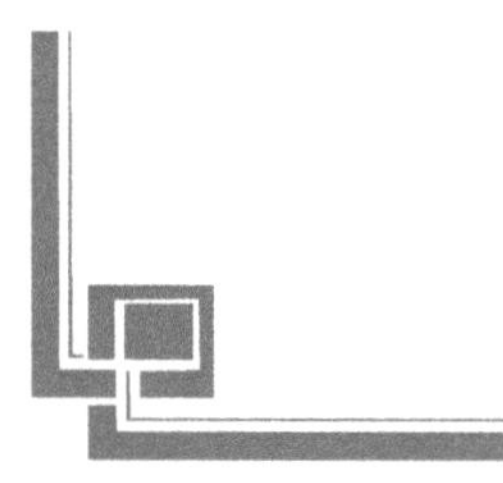

ΘΥ ΙΣ
ΧΣ Ο ΑΓΙΟΣ
ΙΩ·

"Jesue."

In the Arabic Scriptural context of what is called Jesus........."

"Jesue."

"Leopard."

In the Jungle this Leopard lurks unseen from it's Humanistic predators but known vaguely by foreign onlookers that in observe there every move………"

"Leopard."

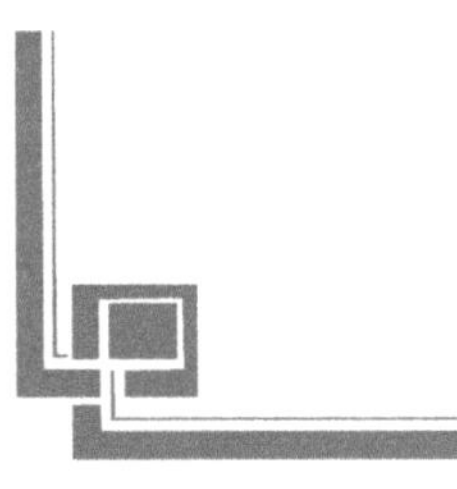

mf
f
cresc.
tr
ff
meno f
sans ralentir
pizz.
arco
pp
cédez un peu
P sub.
pizz.
arco
mp
rall.
a Tempo
surtout, sans ralentir
restez
pp
surtout, sans ralentir
restez III
sur la touche
mf très doux et expr.
sur la t
pp
tr
pizz.
pizz.
mf
pizz.
mf

"Song Walker."

Song written at the expense of fun as the music begin to drum
each sound for it being done.........."

"Song Walker."

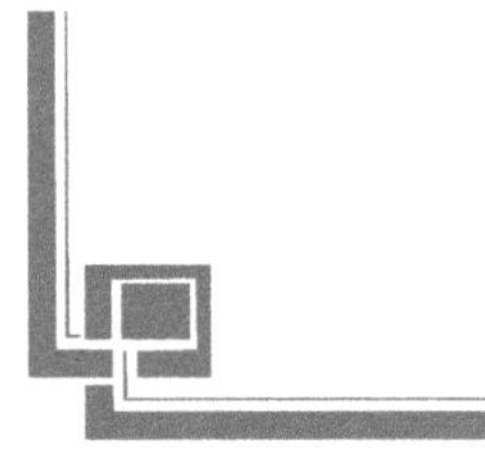

"Morning Talker."

In the Morning they talk as each one review every Literary notion of
Mr. Drummond............"

"Morning Talker."

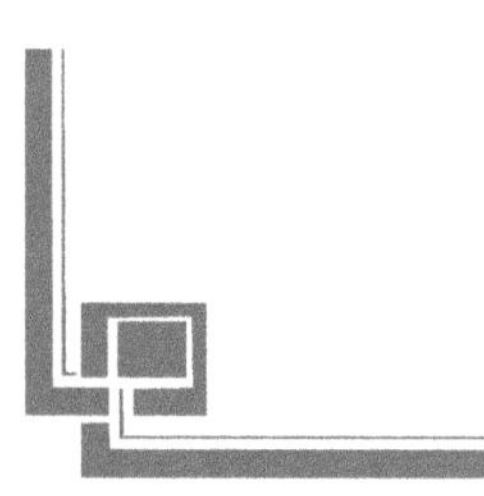

"Night Prayer."

In the Night; I pray as the storm overrides.
the wind and i'm left with the reality of the Moon smiling upon the
Night passive stillness.

"If a woman."

If a woman trust a man; and a Man trust a woman,
we are left with the fact of success with our relationship together.

ZEPPELIN

"Drummond Dollars."

Drummond Literary consummation is consume by threats
made by those who Understand monetary gain............"

"Drummond Dollars."

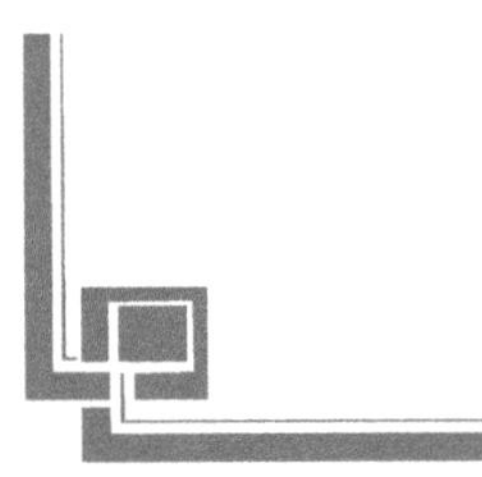

Tropical but wild animal lives in the jungle were happiness is their daily meal............."

"Jaguar."

"Never let a Woman."

Never let a woman use you to pursue the necessity of greatness which upholds Honorary mentions that come from him.

PROCEED   NO
FURTHER

"I Quit."

I Quit from pleasing those who don't Understand what doesn't concern the mere act of Literary greatness they don't know............"

"When a woman lies."

When a woman lies the Truth isn't the reality that come from
those who change............"

"Money Gospel."

Nobody knows which perception cause the mere act of monetary greed to set in concerning the Gospel............"

ZEPPELIN

"Never trust a Woman."

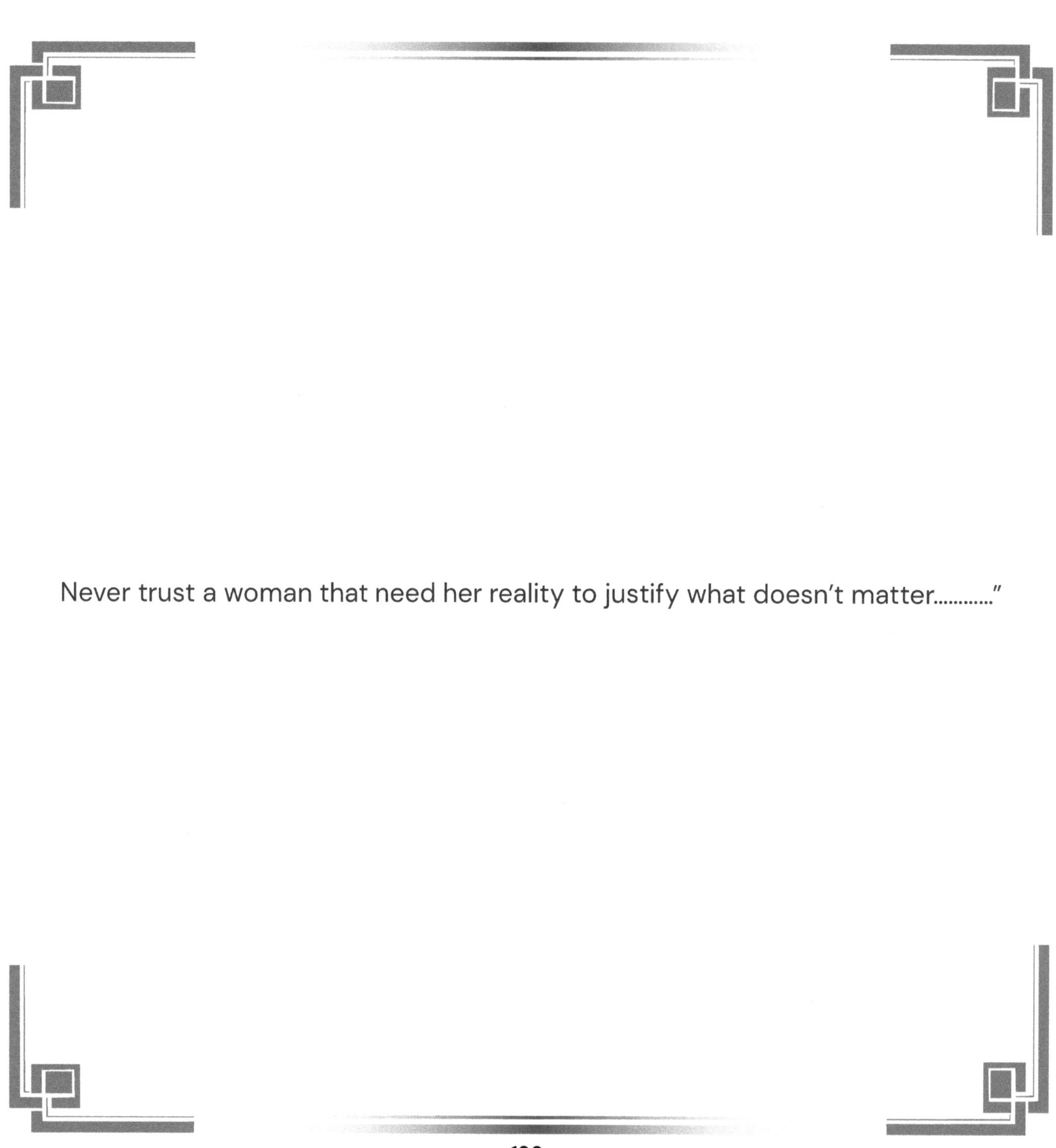

Never trust a woman that need her reality to justify what doesn't matter............"

"Songs of Drummond."

Songs are made by the touch for Musical growth everybody knows that
Drummond is a Kingly Poet…………"

"Songs of Drummond."

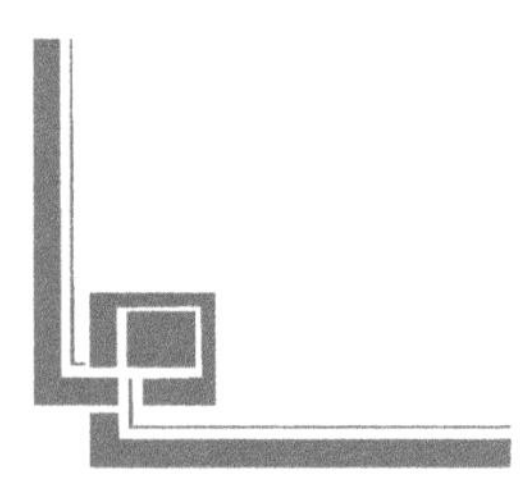

"Scar." II

Literary Touch by the reality for growth nobody knows that Scar is Scarce............"

"Scar."ll

ZEPPELIN

"Angelic Thoughts." II

Angelic Thoughts are made by touch which pushes against the reality of Life............"

“After Evening.”

After the sun goes down the words are sound and
somebody knows he is here............"

"After Evening."

ZEPPELIN

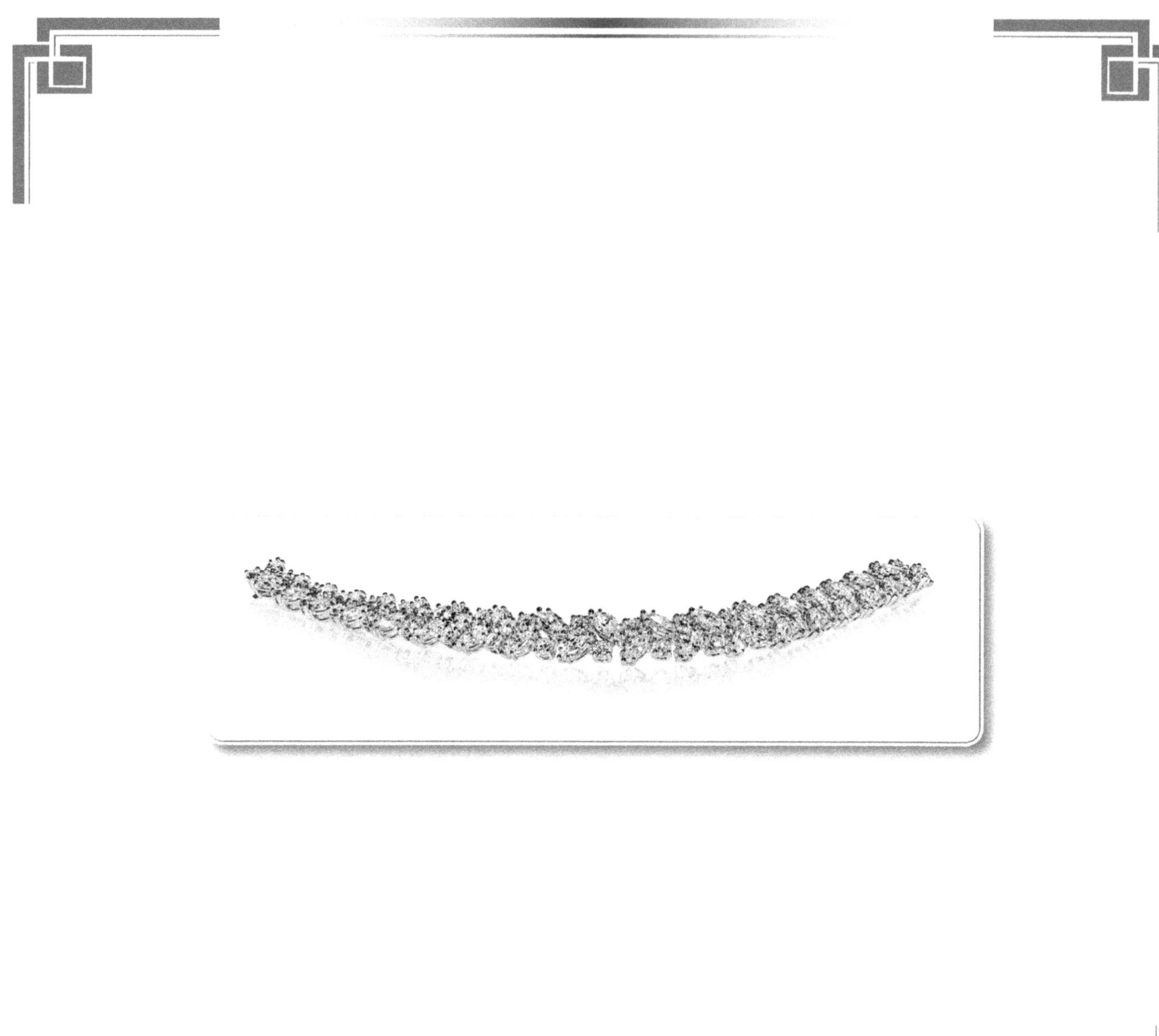

"White Gold."

White but Gold is worn to attract the likes of People who admire his chain.........."

"White Gold."

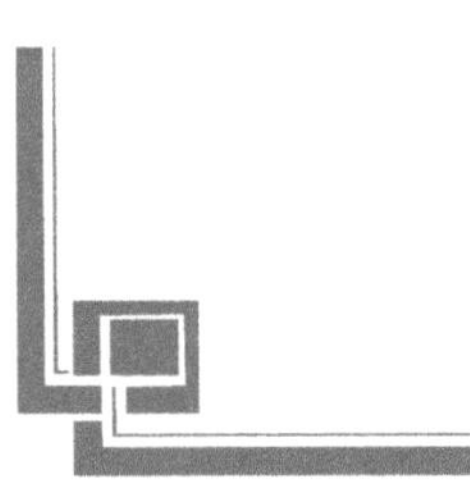

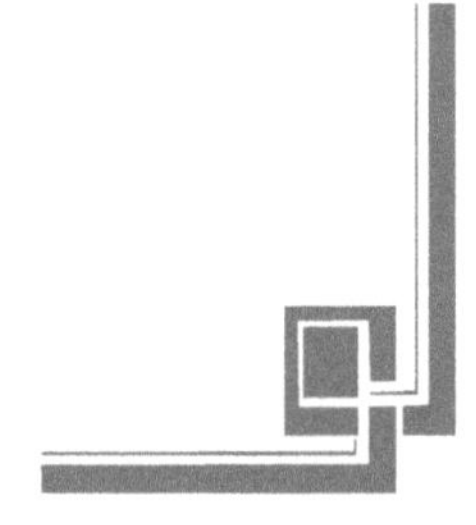

"White Diamond." 11

Cut to Perfection a White Diamond shines ever so brightly
as it is made into a item to be purchase.

"White Diamond."ll

ZEPPELIN

GLOBAL
INTERGOLD
50g
FINE GOLD
999.9
NMR
G00023
GLOBAL
INTERGOLD
OUNCE
GOLD
GLOBAL
INTERGOLD
100g
FINE GOLD
999.9
NMR
G00003

"Dollars as Trees."

Dollars are consume by leafs from trees; we start to see as
paper in written format words are made............"

“Drummone.”

Literature told from a foreign dialect nobody knows that he really cares
Mr. Drummone............"

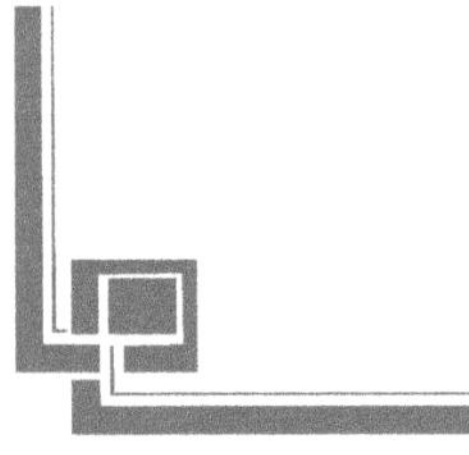

"Purse."

Literary notions told by consummation monetary gain futuristically hold the Purse of Drummond............"

ZEPPELIN

"Vault."

A Vault that contain thy Literary notions that I now
Understand is mine by Thought............"

ZEPPELIN

"Panther."

Black but Beautiful this animal love in the jungle and roam at night............"

"Panther."

ZEPPELIN

NEVER EVER GIVE UP.

“I Never.”

Once inspired by those I'd Literary read know one believed
inspiration came from none............"

"I Never."

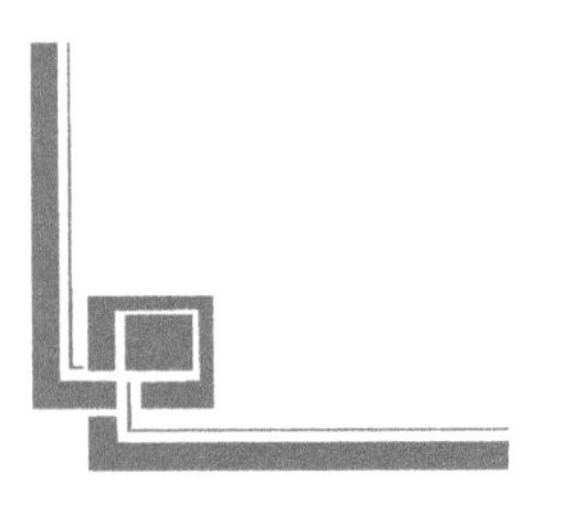

ZEPPELIN

"Musical Inspiration."

Musically inspired by the touch of people who cares about
significance told from inscription tales told............"

"Sardius Diamond."

Rarely significant the stones glimmers without interaction
nobody cares but everybody knows this Sardius Diamond............"

ZEPPELIN

"White Fire as Rain."

White as Fire Rain falls from the sky told by time with Change............"

“Literary Doctor.”

Literary notions consume at the cost of Perfection told by mere acts in
Literal Doctrine documented from Mr. Drummond............"

"Literary Doctor."

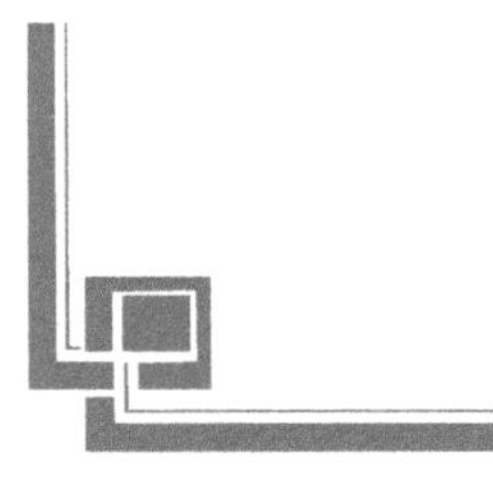

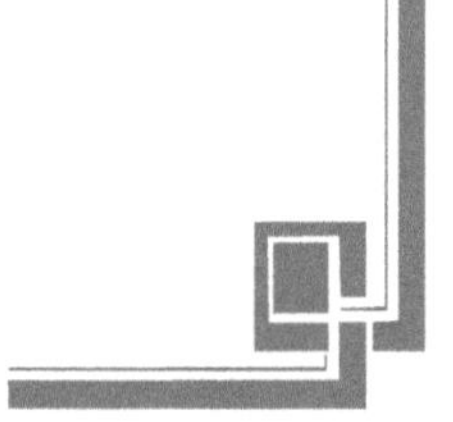

Acknowledgements.

I would like to first Thank God for Blessing me with the Gift of Poetry.
Secondly I want to thank my Mother for being there.
Lastly I appreciate everyone that contributed to this Book.

www.ingramcontent.com/pod-product-compliance
Lightning Source LLC
Chambersburg PA
CBHW041027050726
47599CB00018B/1891